Praise for *Dying: A Natural Passage*

Denys Cope opens our eyes to the spiritual aspects and the wisdom that are inherent in the dying process. As a nurse, she offers us very practical steps in how to enhance the sacredness in dying. Her reassurance that healing can happen in the dying journey brings us hope and meaning.

— Larry Dossey, MD, author of *The Extraordinary Healing Power of Ordinary Things, Healing Beyond the Body,* and *New York Times* bestseller *Healing Words: The Power of Prayer and the Practice of Medicine*

A valuable manual for people who are facing the . . . death of a loved one and should be required reading for anyone involved in the care of the dying. The book is written with deep sensitivity and wisdom and an authenticity that comes from the author's many years of intimate involvement with the dying process.

— Erica Elliott, MD, Family Practice and Environmental Medicine

Denys Cope's *Dying: A Natural Passage* is profound and moving. It allows us to understand the deeper wisdom and compassion in dying and not to fear the process in this sacred time.

— Barbara Dossey, PhD, RN, AHN-BC, FAAN, author of *Florence Nightingale Today: Healing, Leadership, Global Action; Holistic Nursing: A Handbook for Practice;* and *Rituals of Healing*

Refreshing in its honesty and grounded in common sense.

— Pam Nelson, family member

This is a tremendously helpful . . . book, in its simplicity, it's straightforwardness, and the basic information it contains. The process is so medicalized in hospital settings that it is easy to miss the simple and profound reality of this most natural process.
— Marguerite Holmes, MN, PhD, HMC

So clear and easy to read, and yet very moving and profound. These amazing experiences will be of comfort to so many people in their future journeys, and to their loved ones who care for them. If this invaluable information had been available to me thirty years ago, when I started working with hospice patients and families, it would have made a significant difference in my practice.
— Susan Ehret Harlan, RN, CQI/Education Manager,
Home Health Services

Within this book is very poignant and powerful yet simple, straightforward advice.
— Mary Beth Hand, RN, Executive Director, Carlos Otis
Stratton Mountain Clinic

It flows so easily from subject to subject . . . There is such a down-home wisdom that is easily reachable for many.
— Sharon Leftwich, RN, hospice nurse

My father passed away about three years ago. I wish I had read this information . . . then. It could have saved us a lot of worry knowing more about what was happening to him.
— M.W., family member

This book enabled my late wife and me to spend our last two months together living instead of dying.
— Ken Mayer

Denys Cope's words helped us through the most difficult and confusing times human beings can endure—both the dying human, as well as the surviving humans. We are grateful for the assistance during our time of need, and I don't think we could have experienced it as calmly, or as fully, as we did, without the help.
— Susan M. Quirk, family member

When my mother died, your book was invaluable. Knowing what to expect helped me be more present in the moment, and (I hope) helped me be with my mother, and be there for her.
— Lori Allen, family member

Your clarity and forthrightness helped us to know the stages to help our mother better. I am so grateful for that.
— Jan Torgeson, family member

DYING
A NATURAL PASSAGE

DENYS COPE, RN, BSN

Three Whales Publishing, LLC
Santa Fe, New Mexico

Three Whales Publishing, LLC
4524 Calle Turquesa, Santa Fe, NM 87507
www.livingthroughdying.com

Cover photo: © Bill Ross/Corbis
Author photo by Renie Haiduk, Haiduk Photography, Haidukphotography.com, Santa Fe
Book design & typography by Diane Rigoli, www.rigoliartstudio.com, San Francisco

Dying is factually correct, except that names and individual traits have been altered to preserve coherence while protecting privacy. Moreover, the content of this book is provided for educational and informational purposes only and is not intended as a substitute for medical advice. Readers are encouraged to consult a physician on all health matters, especially symptoms that may require medical attention.

Printed in the United States of America on 100% recycled paper.
Library of Congress Cataloging-in-Publication Data
Cope, Denys
    Dying: a natural passage/ Denys Cope. — Santa Fe, NM.: Three Whales
Publishing, 2007
        p. ; cm.
        ISBN-10: 0-9787506-5-9
        ISBN-13: 978-0-9787506-5-7
        Includes bibliographical references and index

    1. Death—Physiological aspects. 2. Death—Psychological aspects
    3. Death—Religious aspects. 4. Grief—Psychological aspects. 5. Bereavement—
Psychological aspects.

BF789.D4 C67 2007   2006910392
155. 9/37—dc22   0704
        10 9 8 7 6 5 4 3 2

CONTENTS

A special acknowledgment of deep appreciation and gratitude to William C. (Bill) Staley and his devoted family—his nieces Dianne Simpson and family, Nina Hill and family, and Jennifer Anderson and family.

Bill died during the creation of this book, and I was deeply touched to participate in his remarkable passage. His journey through the last weeks and days of his life embodied everything I have come to believe and teach about the sacredness, profound blessings, and life-changing mystery available at this time. I am forever honored to have known him and been a part of his dying, as well as his living.

The generosity of Bill's family has certainly contributed to the creation of this book.

Acknowledgments

This book is a result of the constant encouragement of so many supporters to put into print what I have been teaching for years.

First, thank you to all the special souls—family, friends, and especially patients and their families who, in the vulnerable authenticity of the dying experience, taught me the truths of this sacred experience.

My sister, Laura Hess, has been the wind beneath my wings, always believing in me even in my times of procrastination.

My dear friend Pepper Sbarbaro, my lifelong soul sister and confidant who has held for me through thick and thin.

My southern soul sister Rebecca Skeele who, in deep friendship, has been the patient, loving way-shower for my Spirit's journey and the creative, focused coach and loving way-shower for this book.

Chelle Thompson, valued friend and editor, who has been a steady, inspired presence providing the first forum for me to step into my soul's calling to teach about death and dying and who has given me years of support including skillful editing and an eventual artful presence on her website, www .InspirationLine.com.

Henrietta Cope, my stepmother, who in her nineties shows me how to live through the deaths of many loved ones and still embrace life full of grace and vitality.

My extended family, both living and gone, who teach the value of the continuity of loving throughout life and death.

All of my dear, dear friends, too numerous to name, who have been in my corner chanting "You Go Girl." Without their love and support this book would not be.

I also want to thank the special angels who have been part of the actual creation of this book:

Mimi Thompson Breed, lifelong friend who painstakingly first put my thoughts on dying into print.

DYING: A NATURAL PASSAGE

Ben Colodzin, PhD, the inspired interviewer who put my thoughts into publication, giving me the foundation for this book, and later sent a generous guardian angel my way.

Amanda Coslor, that guardian angel whose gift affirmed a level of support for this book beyond my imagination.

Barbara M. Dossey, PhD, who lovingly encouraged me to grow the interview into a separate creation.

Alan and Becky Stoker and Sally Dessauer, who gifted me with the time that allowed the fruition of this dream.

David Christel and Gussie Fauntleroy, who contributed their talents as editors to heartfully and skillfully capture and develop the essence of my words and thoughts.

Rhonda Avidon and Janet Van Sky, whose eagle eyes brought a polish that allows these words to shine.

Ellen Kliener, editor par excellence, who artfully crafted the ultimate flow and coherence on these pages.

ACKNOWLEDGMENTS

Jytte Lokvig, whose experience in publishing, enthusiasm, and generous spirit were invaluable as she walked beside me in this creation.

Diane Rigoli, whose creative talent as a graphic designer as well as steady patience were so integral to bringing beauty to this book.

Death ends a life,
not a relationship.

— MORRIE SCHWARTZ

—⟨∞∞⟩—

Introduction

We, the living (which we all are until we take our last breath), owe it to ourselves, our loved ones, and our society to learn about the process of dying. We need to understand that death is a natural part of life. In fact, we need to become as familiar with dying as we have with pregnancy, labor, and birth.

There was a time when pregnancy was not openly discussed, and certainly nursing mothers were seldom seen in public. We did not see pregnant women portrayed on television until *I Love Lucy*. It was all a mystery kept behind closed doors. Now, pregnant women are often viewed on television, and actresses are seen fully pregnant in skintight, revealing dresses. In sitcoms, we have seen a woman's water breaking and even witnessed certain aspects of labor and birth. Mothers now nurse their children in public. It has become a normal part of our culture. It is out of the closet.

Now death must come out of the closet. As a society, is it not time for us to stop pretending it does not exist for us? Death is not a failure, and we are all going to experience it. We are part of nature's cycle, just as is every living organism on earth. We are born, we live, and we die. Ideally, we will become as familiar with the stages of dying as we are with those of pregnancy and birthing. Then, when we are faced with death in our personal lives, we will read about and learn the finer details of the process. We will gather support around ourselves just as we do when pregnancy becomes a personal reality. In this way, shame, fear, and uncertainty are less likely to arise.

As we learn to accept dying as a normal, expected part of life, we demystify it and understand the hard work it is, as well as embrace the gifts that accompany it. When we learn how to best be with each other during this most poignant of times, to offer true peace and comfort, we will have changed ourselves as individuals and as a society.

Too often, we are not comfortable around a dying person. We are afraid for many reasons but most frequently because we are dealing with the unknown. We are not sure what to say, what to do, or how to be with someone who is dying, afraid that we will say or do the wrong thing or somehow cause harm. We frequently believe something is going wrong and we are responsible for fixing it. Many times people who are dying feel guilty for having or causing their illness. They may feel shame for being ill or letting loved ones down or creating discomfort in other people. They may fear suffering or being a burden. And they might experience grief at leaving loved ones, or anger at having life and loved ones taken away. These feelings are all a natural reaction to a process that, for the most part, is foreign and therefore is often entered into blindly and with many misconceptions.

Sadly, although most Americans express a desire to die at home, only 30 to 35 percent actually do.[1] The remainder die in accidents or in the hospital, either due to irreversible conditions that have arisen, or by choice, for one reason or another. Sometimes this is because family members are frightened and feel totally ill equipped to care for their loved ones. Even when there is some acceptance of death, many people feel completely inadequate to deal with the process. It is hard to be around pain, to see apparent discomfort and suffering, and to feel so helpless. Occasionally, being in the hospital is the choice of the dying person, who sees those fears and does not want to be a burden to family members who are already overwhelmed. Fortunately the steady increase in hospice care is making it possible for more people each year to die at home or in a hospice inpatient facility.

As a registered nurse since the midsixties and a hospice nurse for more than half of that time, I have learned that one of the most important parts of hospice care is teaching family and friends about the dying process, to allow them to become comfortable being with and caring for their loved ones.

With education and support, especially from hospice, a peaceful death at home or in an inpatient hospice facility can be facilitated. And when a person does die in a hospital or nursing home, with awareness, that death can also happen in as peaceful and supportive an environment as possible.

What helps is to become familiar with the actual dying process, the physiology of it, and the spiritual aspects that emerge, to know what is really going on. This book describes what happens when people are counting their life in weeks or months rather than years. It is based on what I have learned from the many individuals with whom I have been involved during the last days of their lives.

Taking care of a loved one who is dying presents some of the most difficult, demanding, and rewarding work we will ever do. Always the challenges are unique—to the course of the disease, our loved ones' relationship to their own death, and our connection with them. Understanding how to be with loved ones in their last days is one of the most life-affirming—and life- and death-altering gifts we can give them and ourselves.

Dying is absolutely safe.

— RAM DASS

PART I

About Dying

Overview

It is most important to know that the dying process is not something to be feared. It is a very normal, natural, exquisitely well-orchestrated physical and spiritual experience, just like the pregnancy, labor, and birth process that it parallels. There is a pregnancy to the dying process, a labor, a transition phase, and then the "deathing," instead of birthing.

No matter what brings one to the dying process, whether it is cancer, old age, lung disease, heart disease, Alzheimer's, or any other disease, the process eventually becomes the same, except in the cases of sudden or traumatic death. The dying process is like being in a funnel; everybody comes to this time from different conditions, and then they move into the same physiological process. This becomes a very recognizable phenomenon.

Like labor and birth, the dying process can vary from an easy, quick experience to a very long and difficult one to a rich and peaceful experience, or any combination of these. The experience ultimately is unique to each person, just as our birth is.

Throughout the dying process, a person naturally begins to do things that conserve energy. Our body is programmed for survival, to live as long as it can and to support life as long as it can. Energy conservation is one of the ways it does this. We eat less and lighter food because our body cannot utilize the food as well. We do less and less physically as we turn inward toward an internal focus. Very often these same changes in lifestyle are also common in elder hood, and, in themselves, they do not necessarily indicate someone has started to die. It is when several factors come together that one can see, most often in retrospect, that the person had been in the early stages of dying for a while.

One patient, Elaine, told me that, in looking back, she realized she had had cancer for much longer than she had known. It was early springtime when I met her, and she had been newly diagnosed with pancreatic cancer. Elaine said: "You know, now that I think about it, last winter I didn't feel like going to church as much. And for the first time in my life I didn't feel like building a fire this winter." She just did not have the energy to do the things in life that normally mattered to her. It was only in hindsight that she could see she was withdrawing from the world and spending more and more time resting and conserving energy. It was also interesting that when, a month before she was diagnosed, Elaine did find the strength to go out with her son and granddaughters during their visit from Hong Kong because they nurtured her energetically.

Another important awareness to hold is that throughout the dying process, we, the caregivers, tend to project on our dying loved ones what we think they are going through. Trying to put ourselves in their place, we invariably imagine they must be in discomfort or pain because it looks like it to us. In fact, the dying person is usually undergoing a very different experience of his or her body, one that often does not involve the level of suffering we believe is happening.

Many people associate dying with pain. They think the more pain someone is in, the closer to death he must be. They do not realize that increased physical pain is associated with the advancing illness, not dying, and can in fact be effectively managed. Death, on the other hand, has its own timing, regardless of the presence or absence of pain.

This is not to say there is not pain and suffering during this time, because there can be. But this relates to the illness, not to dying. The actual dying process, which entails the closing down of the body's functions, is not painful.

Societal Views

As a society, it is our challenge to understand that death is not a failure. Death may come as the result of actions or events that appear to have failed, but death itself is not a failure. It is something we each will go through, and it is as much a part of life as birth.

We all have our time, and yes, most of us would fight for life if we were diagnosed with a terminal illness. We would do everything within our power to facilitate a cure. However, once we had given every effort and it had become clear a cure was not happening, then it would be time to look at the end of our life. Even if a cure gave one a second chance, it would still be time to consider the end of our life. After all, it is going to happen at some point.

When we turn and face our mortality, we are making a difficult choice. Yet repeatedly, when people make that choice, it is because they have done everything they could to cure their illness but it has become too much and thus death has become something to surrender to.

Ken Wilber wrote a remarkable book about his wife's dying process, *Grace and Grit,* which captures this very movingly. One can do all the spiritual work and all the physical work, yet if the time has come to make the transition from this world, then this fact must be accepted on some level, even if it is only in the unconscious. In Wilber's book, his wife did all she could to heal from her cancer over several years, and then one day she said, essentially, "Enough. I have given it my all. I am tired." And she surrendered to her dying process. By dying when and as she did, she left a gift that helped the world become a better place. I have certainly learned a great deal from her death and what her husband wrote about it.

In many cultures, especially the Eastern traditions, meditating on one's death is part of a daily spiritual practice. As a result, when a person's time comes, it is something very familiar and known, and it is therefore not likely to engender deep fear. This is certainly true of the Buddhist traditions. Among others, His Holiness the Dalai Lama, spiritual leader of the Tibetan Buddhists, speaks of this practice.

In addition, many indigenous cultures have, as a right of passage from adolescence into adulthood, a ritual in which people actually experience their own death on a mystical level. This is done with the understanding that as one faces one's fear of death, there will no longer be a fear of living life fully.

There is a powerful video produced by Eliot Rosen, a hospice social worker entitled *Conscious Dying: Preparing Now for a Healing Passage, the Transition We Call Death*. In it are interviews with well-known figures in the field of conscious dying, including Elisabeth Kübler-Ross, Ram Dass, and

Stephen Levine, as well as interviews with people who were dying and people who have had near-death and out-of-body experiences.

In this video, we learn about the Aboriginal people of Australia and their traditions surrounding life and death. In that culture, when a person is born, the tribe surrounds the baby and celebrates, and the first thing the baby is told is, "We love you and support you on your journey." The person grows and lives a full life. Finally, when the person realizes it is time to die, a party is held, like a graduation celebration. The last thing the person is told is, "We love you and support you on your journey." Then the person is left alone. He or she sits down and within a matter of minutes is able to intentionally close down the body and die. Now that is the ultimate in conscious dying.

This ability is also a well-documented phenomenon among Tibetan, Hindu, and Zen masters as compiled by Sushila Blackman in her remarkable book *Graceful Exits: How Great Beings Die*, which recounts the death stories of 108 spiritual masters.

We have heard of other indigenous cultures in which it was traditional for elders to leave the tribe and go out into the wilds alone when they knew it was their time to die. Perhaps we modern folk tend to imagine the elders went out there and were eaten by animals, froze to death, or starved to death, or in some other way went through great physical suffering. Yet I have come to understand, as I learn more about indigenous cultures, that it is more likely they knew of a way to bring about their own death naturally. With an intuitive knowledge, they understood it was time, knew where to go, knew what to do, and did it.

If this capacity exists among some people, then it must be available to all of us. One thing seems certain: it requires a strong connection to a spiritual source and the ability to enter into a deep meditative state. Thankfully, in this day and age it is not necessary to separate oneself from loved ones to die. On the other hand, we, as a culture and individually, have a long way to go before death is integrated into our everyday life as a normal, natural part of living.

Relationships – A Time for Healing

The dying often go through dramatic changes in the way they live their lives when they know they have little time left. One fellow I took care of, Paul, was among the angriest people I have ever met. He was fifty-one and dying of bladder cancer. With a wry sense of humor, he said of his disease: "Well, what do you expect from someone who has been pissed off all his life?" And evidently he truly had been angry for all his life. Paul was a complex, sometimes delightful, often very difficult person to be around. He was experiencing quite a bit of pain in the course of his disease. To help manage this pain, pain specialist physicians were continually involved in his care. Paul would get one kind of pain under control and another would pop up. We would work on that one, then another would develop; he could never get comfortable for long.

After several weeks of this pattern, it became clear to those of us caring for Paul, including his partner, that at some deep unconscious level Paul needed his pain and he needed to suffer. It was, we supposed, part of the way he was trying to atone for a lifelong pattern of what he saw as pretty poor behavior on his part with many people.

The last three weeks of Paul's life were very interesting. His twenty-five-year-old son, John, and Paul's partner, Sarah, did not get along; they were like oil and water. Paul finally requested a family conference and asked me to mediate the meeting. A few minutes into the discussion, he said to John and Sarah, "You know, up until now I've been sick, but something has shifted and I know I'm dying and we don't have time for this anymore. We have got to learn how to get along." From that moment on, the peace that enveloped their household was remarkable. Paul really seemed to stop suffering. And while he had a tube in his kidneys and still needed quite a bit of pain medication, he had come to a place of incredible peace. In his last three weeks of life, Paul became a very soft and loving partner and father. We can change and grow, even in our final days, hours, and minutes.

Transforming Guilt

So often when we are diagnosed with a serious or life-threatening illness we think something has gone terribly wrong and wonder: "What have I done to deserve this? How can I fight it?" How many times have you heard someone say, "I am going to beat this"? Yet there is a different, more gentle, more loving way to be with ourselves and our illness than to see it as a punishment or something to fight.

Stephen Levine describes this beautifully in Eliot Rosen's previously mentioned video. He says people get caught up in the idea that we are responsible for our life-threatening illnesses. To be responsible for an illness means that you have somehow caused it. The underlying message is that if you just do your spiritual work, tend to your emotional clearing, eat healthy food, and do everything right, the illness will disappear and you will not have to die.

The belief that illness results from something you did wrong leads to feelings of guilt. Seen differently, the minute you start thinking you are responsible for your illness, Levine notes, you have made an enemy of it and begin to send fear to that illness. He concludes, "We are not responsible *for* our illness, we're responsible *to* our illness."[1] Therefore, if illness shows up, we must ask ourselves what it is we need to do for ourselves in response to it. That way we can move in concert with the illness and see the lessons it holds for us, see the experiences that are there for us and for those we love.

The reality is that all of us on this earth right now will die within the next 110 to 130 years. Death is going to be part of our experience. So what are our choices in response to this reality? We can feel *responsible for* our situation and say, "Oh my God, I caused my cancer because I ate the wrong thing" or "I'm sick because I'm angry at this person or because I haven't been spiritual enough." We can be like Paul, who said, "I've been pissed off all my life, no wonder I have bladder cancer." He believed he was being punished and had created the whole situation. Now illness can indeed serve as a metaphor, and certain lifestyles do contribute to the development of particular diseases, but Paul wasn't speaking in metaphorical terms; he was feeling *responsible for* his disease.

Our other choice, as Levine says, is to become *responsible to* the situation in which we find ourselves. This means saying to ourselves, "Okay, I've got this illness. Now what can I do to gain the most from whatever this illness has to teach me?"

Further, we can put another question to ourselves: "Is this a time for me to really, in a heartfelt way, say, 'Thank you, God'?" I recall a woman who had cancer, and as a response she understood it was time for her to reprioritize and reorder her life, which she did. Subsequently, her cancer went into remission. Later, the cancer came back a couple of times, and she said, "You know, it's been a real friend to me, because it keeps coming back and reminding me, 'Which way are you walking? What life choices are you making?'"

Cancer has become her barometer. Eventually, it will probably become her teacher about how to leave this world. So, feeling *responsible for* leads to feeling guilty, as though you must get rid of things, while feeling *responsible to* means looking at how you can respond to whatever has come into your life.

Dying is a personal experience,
not a medical problem.

PART II

Stages of Dying

Pregnancy of Dying

The beginning signs of pregnancy often go unrecognized, especially with the first experience, and it is only in hindsight that the mother is able to acknowledge that the indications have been there for a while. The same is true at the end of life, So often, it is only retrospectively that the family or the person dying is able to recognize that the process has been unfolding for a while.

PHYSICAL NOURISHMENT

Many people ask, "How do I know if my loved one has begun dying?" One of the first considerations is whether the person has changed his or her relationship to food. In the early stage of pregnancy, a new mother's first clue that something is occurring is a change in her relationship to food, which is usually marked by morning sickness. In the beginning of dying, the change in one's relationship to food is marked by a diminished appetite. In both cases, decreased energy is usually part of the picture as well.

Because the early stages of dying are marked by loss of appetite and energy, it is very important to work with one's doctor and look at the whole picture. Loss of appetite and low energy can also be signs of other physical problems, including depression. A medical examination, along with any tests that are indicated, is an important part of determining one's actual state of health.

When dying begins, the body naturally withdraws from nourishment, from that which sustains physical life. The person, over time, is switching from a physical energy source to a spiritual energy source, so usually there is a natural diminishing of appetite with accompanying weight loss.

There are many physical reasons for this change in eating habits. People eat less and lighter food because their bodies cannot digest nutrients as well as before. In addition to losing weight, their metabolism slows down, their activity level decreases, and they grow weaker. Significant weight loss is one of the criteria considered when a person is being assessed for hospice.

The body has a wisdom of its own. When a person has a growing cancer, much of the food taken in feeds the cancer. When the appetite diminishes and less is eaten, the cancer receives less fuel, and in a basic way, does not grow as quickly. Nevertheless, it is very important that people with cancer not be afraid to eat. In fact, for anyone pursuing curative treatment, nourishment is vital to support healing. For a person moving into the dying process with cancer, food becomes a quality of life rather than a quantity of life issue. If the person has an appetite and feels like eating, food is to be enjoyed, not feared.

When a person has advanced cardiac or lung disease, the body wants to conserve energy, so the tired heart or lungs do not have to work any harder than necessary. Eating and digesting food takes energy. When the appetite and eating decrease, the body can conserve whatever energy is available for the more important job of keeping the heart beating or taking the next breath.

When people are dying and losing their appetite, we often project onto them our need for them to eat. We want them to eat because feeding our loved ones is our way of nurturing them. Normally if people are not eating very much, it means they are sick. We want them to eat because if they do, we believe, they will be "better," and they won't die.

As we watch people eat progressively less and less, we may be afraid they are "starving to death." The truth is, people who are dying have a natural and gradual loss of appetite and do not need the same quantity of food. Often they will tell you clearly that they just don't have much of an appetite. They may occasionally have a craving for some food and will enjoy it—in small amounts. At other times, they think they want something and may even bring it up to their mouths, but then they stop. They just are unable to put it into their mouths. Sometimes they know that if they eat it, they will get sick. Other times they just suddenly become aware they don't want it. Eating, again, at this point is about quality of life, not quantity.

Sometimes people who are dying may eat anyway, in order to take care of loved ones who need them to eat. When they do eat, however, they often become nauseated because their metabolism and digestion have slowed down and they truly do not need the food.

The father of Kay, a friend of mine, was dying. Kay's mother was having a very hard time accepting his decline. She kept encouraging him to eat. This was her way of loving him.

Once Kay's father had finished eating and his wife had left the room, he would ask Kay to clean his dentures, which of course she did. When he took them out, she saw that her father had packed all the food on top of the dentures as a way of appearing to eat without really doing so. He knew how much it meant to his wife to see him eat.

The work of the family, therefore, is to have the courage and wisdom to listen to our dying loved ones, let them set the pace, and respond sensitively and appropriately. When we do this, we are faced with accepting the fact that we can no longer nurture them through food. We need to be aware that we are also acknowledging that they are dying. This can be a very difficult point in the early stages of the process. As we experience the grief that comes with that reality, we need to look for other ways to nurture and relate to our dying loved ones. We also need to find ways to nurture and sustain ourselves as we go through this very challenging and often difficult work with them.

As people are withdrawing from food, they move away from heavier, harder-to-digest foods, even foods that used to be their favorites. The first things to go are meats and fats, cheeses, and fried foods. More easily digested foods such as potatoes, rice, toast, and eggs become more appealing. Then, at some point, they may only want soft foods, such as applesauce and yogurt, and perhaps ice cream, milkshakes, and health drinks. Soon, they may only want juices, then only Gatorade and water, maybe ice chips, and then just sips of water. Finally they stop drinking altogether. When they reach this stage, they usually have three to five days left. Many people will lock their lips at this point, and will not allow you to put anything in their mouth. On the other hand, some people continue to eat until the day they die. This whole process can go very quickly or very slowly. Just like labor and birth, it is entirely individualized.

As the dying person gradually withdraws from eating and drinking, the question of a feeding tube and intravenous drips comes up as part of the family's desire to keep their loved one comfortable. This is often the case when family members are afraid the patient is dying of starvation or thirst or both. It is so very important to realize that the withdrawal from food and fluids is a natural process that actually supports the dying person's comfort. It does not create suffering because the dying body's needs do not entail physical healing and ongoing life.

The withdrawal from food and fluids in our loved one's last days has a sedative effect leading to an enhanced sense of well-being and diminished illness-related pain. As the body withdraws from nutritional sustenance it naturally goes into a fasting mode. Fasting generally supports one of two purposes. The first purpose most people think of is cleansing, which creates its own sense of well-being, but an additional reason for fasting is enhancement of spiritual experiences. Therefore, as the dying person moves into a fasting mode, he or she also is able to open to an altered state of consciousness that promotes an inner experience of disconnectedness from the body and facilitates connection to the spiritual realm. Thus, withdrawal from food and fluids actually supports the dying process.

Attempting to override this biochemical state in the hope of providing comfort actually creates the opposite effect. Giving intravenous fluids at this point will bring them back into their body and out of the natural comfort-creating altered state. With the reconnection to the physical, they once again become more aware of any physical discomfort.

Meanwhile the body, which is shutting down, cannot effectively use these fluids, which are then likely to lead to swelling in the body and eventually may fill the lungs and cause respiratory distress.

The challenging work of caregivers is to learn to trust the body's wisdom, respond to the needs of their loved one rather than to their own projections of what is needed, and take care of themselves during this profound transition.

When nourishment cannot take place through food and fluids, there are other ways of being with, nurturing, and sharing love with them. These include playing and listening to music together, reading to them, talking with them, going through photo albums, looking at memorabilia, or simply sitting quietly in the room.

SPIRITUAL NOURISHMENT

It is important to address the dying person's spiritual beliefs or questions. The person may have been raised Christian, Jewish, Muslim, or in some other formal religion, and been away from that tradition for many years. Yet when it comes time to die people may want to reconnect with their religion. As one woman put it, "Well, I think I'd like to talk to a minister, just in case there really is a God and I need to be on his good side."

Even when a person has not followed any particular religion, it is still natural, especially at this stage in life, to have questions and concerns about spiritual matters, perhaps about the meaning of her life. It is important to explore these concerns with the dying person and to provide any support she requests in this area.

The chaplains and spiritual care coordinators on the hospice team are experts at supporting the dying and their loved ones from a nondenominational viewpoint in such situations. Hospice staff also work closely with various spiritual leaders, such as pastors, priests, and rabbis in the community, to respond to the needs of the dying and their families.

The use of rituals aligned with the dying person's belief system can be powerful at this time. Some traditions, for example, encourage the use of oils, incense, particular prayers, sacred music, or special readings to reinforce the spiritually nourishing environment.

TURNING INWARD

Much of the work of dying is an internal, intimately personal process. When people are first faced with the fact that they are counting their life in months, weeks, and days, rather than years, they naturally become reflective.

Consequently, another notable change that happens as one enters the dying process is a gradual withdrawal from the outer world and a turning inward. There is a process of disconnecting from things social, a letting go of out-in-the-world activities and connections. Rarely do people have energy for this kind of focus in their last days.

One of the things people do is to start taking stock of their lives and relationships. They ask themselves, "What has my life meant? Does anything feel unfinished?" They begin to think about the things they have not done, relationships that may not feel complete, or relationships they wish were somehow different. There is an acute awareness of needing to become current with loved ones and to attend to unfinished business. The time that is left becomes very precious.

Very stoic, private people sometimes feel uncomfortable sharing their inner reflections with others.

In such instances the caregiver might gently invite the dying person to give voice to his or her inner thoughts and experiences, while always letting the dying person take the lead.

A wonderful way to support this introspective work is through a life review: talking with them about the times that meant the most to them, going through photo albums and encouraging them to tell stories about the photos, asking them to tell stories about the most important times in their life, and asking who are the significant people they recall. It is also valuable to ask questions such as, "What are some of the things you are glad or feel blessed about that were or are in your life? What are some regrets you might have? How have you dealt with the disappointments in your life? Do you feel complete? If not, what would help you feel complete?"

Sometimes this introspective work can mean helping them finish a project such as a book, memoirs, a quilt, or a photo album. One fellow I knew just wanted to get home from the hospital so he could do nothing more than organize his tackle box one last time.

As well as being reflective, the dying person gradually withdraws, spending more time with those who are most important and more time "resting." Dying people's relationships change in layers. The first layer affected is that of social connections. People stop having energy for those with whom they do not have deep relationships. Next to be affected, as energy decreases, is their close circle of friends, those who are dear to them, but who are not among their core relationships. Eventually, the only people they have energy to be with are those core people who constitute their family—both literally and in a deep loving sense. These are the people for whom they do not have to put on a social face, the ones whose love sustains and nurtures them. Throughout the dying process, it is natural to conserve energy.

Peter was forty-two and dying of liver cancer. He actually had a gathering of those people who meant a great deal to him, with whom he knew he would no longer have the energy to spend time. As the party progressed, Peter lay on a chaise lounge, and one by one his friends came to sit and spend time with him, to share appreciations and say good-bye. It was an extraordinarily touching and direct way of honoring the people who were dear to him while creating space for the time he knew he would need—to be with his wife and himself—in his final days.

As people who are dying withdraw from their broader, external social life, and turn to a deeper, internal personal life, more and more time is spent resting and sleeping. Naps become more frequent and longer, and time with loved ones becomes shorter and more precious.

The person spends more time doing what we, on the outside, think is "just" sleeping. That's how it appears to us as nap times increase. So often the family says, "Oh, he just sleeps all the time. We cannot get him to do anything anymore." The truth is, the person is busy doing important internal work, the work of dying. Dying is hard work, and the business of introspection is done both while awake and asleep, as well as in states of altered consciousness. Dreams continue to be a source of processing and healing. In addition, the dying person enters into states of expanded consciousness and is able to have experiences and insights that support the process.

This introspective work takes place on many levels. As one gets closer to actually dying, there is an experience of seeing or being aware of the "other side." Entering a place of expanded awareness and altered consciousness, people start to become aware beyond the physical level. They begin to travel in their inner world, often visually seeing where they are going. They go into another realm or reality and come back, go and come back. This has been reported by the dying and their families repeatedly, regardless of cultural, religious, or spiritual backgrounds.

People often ask me, "Well, what if you don't believe in that kind of stuff?" In response, I tell the story of Will, a wonderful man and a well-known, much-loved botanist. He was very much the scientist. When I first met him, he was adamant about only believing in the physical world, in things that could be measured and tested and seen. We would have long, philosophical discussions on such things.

As he grew close to the end of his life, he seemed to be taking an inordinate amount of time to die. I say "seemed" because, in truth, people die according to their own perfect timing. All of us who were caring for Will—his family and hospice staff—were projecting upon him what we believed his situation to be, that his quality of life had gone. He was relatively young, in his early fifties, and had prostate cancer. He had a catheter. He was bleeding from his urinary tract, so he was weak with anemia; his lower body was very puffy and swollen with edema (extra fluid in his tissues); he was too weak to walk and needed help with all his toileting; he was often constipated and, at times, was in pain. We could see him becoming thinner and thinner, and closer and closer to the end, and we as hospice caregivers, thought, "This guy is suffering, why doesn't he just let go? What is going on? Why is he hanging on?"

At one point, his hospice nurse said to him, "Will, is there anything that you are afraid of? Anything that is keeping you here?" This is something to explore with people when they seem to be hanging on: whether there is anything they are afraid of, or if there is any unfinished business or something they are waiting for. He said, "Oh no, I'm not afraid. I've been given the gift of seeing where I'm going, and it's so warm and so beautiful; it's just that I don't want to leave here yet." He, the scientist, was having an experience of something beyond the physical, in spite of his beliefs up to that time.

He dearly loved his current partner, his ex-wife, and his daughter, and they were all there with him— his three favorite women. It was a time of deep intimacy, and he was not quite ready to leave them.

It was a real lesson for us as caregivers. We realized that we had been projecting onto him a poor quality of life, while he, in his view, still had such extraordinary quality of life that he wanted to stay as long as possible.

When I spoke with Will's partner five years later, she said, "I just want you to know that was a very special time." She told me that Will, who had lived a very full life, had said to her when he was close to the end, "I am happier than I have ever been in my life." He was quite a teacher for all of us.

PAIN AND SYMPTOM CONTROL

One of the first things to address in creating comfort and quality of life for the dying person's remaining time is to be sure there is sufficient pain control. Hospice physicians and nurses are experts at pain and symptom control. With physical discomfort, quality of life is greatly affected, and suffering is present. Without adequate comfort, it is very difficult to address any of the other areas of the dying process.

Very often, by the time people come to hospice they have been on inadequate pain or symptom control. Sometimes, if it is very late in the dying process, providing adequate pain control is all that is needed to allow the person to let go and die. When this happens, loved ones often think that maybe the stronger, or new, medicine, especially if it is morphine, killed the person. Actually quite the opposite is true. Pain tends to keep a person in their body, and adequate pain relief allows them to relax and let go. Even when people have stopped eating and drinking, medicines can be administered without IVs or injections. Medicine can be given sublingually (under the tongue, or inside the cheek), transdermally (rubbed on the skin, or in a patch that allows it to be absorbed through the skin), rectally, or via the nasal passage. The hospice doctors, nurses, and your physician will help determine your needs as the dying progresses.

When attempting to create comfort, morphine is one of the primary medications to be considered. This is an invaluable medication that is rarely used soon enough. So often the patient or family members or physicians are afraid of the problem of addiction.

Out of this fear, many people believe morphine should be saved "until it is really needed."

In reality, as long as there is pain or trouble breathing and morphine is used to alleviate the distress, it is not being used in an addictive way. Drug abusers use morphine or other addictive substances in order to alter their consciousness, often as a way of coping with emotional difficulties. Yes, there will probably be a gradual need to increase the dose of morphine during end-of-life care, but that is not because the person is becoming addicted. Rather, it is because the condition creating the discomfort is advancing, causing increasing pain. There is also a tolerance to the medication that develops over time, which requires a gradual increase in dosage.

Basically, there are three different kinds of pain:

• Visceral pain: the pain created by disease in the internal organs and structures. It is not specific to one area and is usually described as pressure-like, deep squeezing.

- Neurological pain: the pain most often seen with advanced cancer or advanced neurological disease. Usually this type is described as a "stabbing," "prickling," or "burning sensation" caused by pressure on the nerves.

- Somatic pain: the pain occurring in the musculo-skeletal tissues. At the end of life this is commonly called bone pain. It is most often the result of a cancer spreading to the bones and is usually described as "dull" or "aching" but localized.

For each of these kinds of pain, there are different types of medications that are most effective. The physician will know which medications are indicated. What is important is to have prescribed the right type of medicine and the right dosage for sufficient pain control. This will make all the difference in the quality of life dying people experience during the remainder of their time.

TALKING ABOUT DYING

A question often asked by family members is "Does my loved one know she or he is dying?" Determining whether or not someone is aware of his or her impending death is not easy. Elaine did not know she was terminally ill until after her diagnosis, at which point she could see the signs had been there for some time. Other people have an intuitive sense of their approaching death, sometimes even before they are given a prognosis. What we realize in hospice is that in the last days, if not weeks, of life, dying people usually know they are approaching death, whether they talk about it or not. Sometimes they refrain from speaking about it to spare their family from "facing needless suffering"; other times, it is because they are not ready to deal with it.

Sometimes family, friends or caregivers avoid the topic of approaching death because they do not know what to say or how to say it. If you or your loved one has not brought up the subject of dying, a trusted doctor or one of the hospice staff can be asked to support initiation of a discussion, after which the conversation might flow easily. If it does not, there is no need for concern. What is most helpful is to provide gentle openings for the topic to come up and then respect the desires and comfort level of the person who is approaching the end of life.

FEAR OF DYING

When first faced with the fact they are dying, many people experience a tremendous amount of fear. Often, I am told, it is not death but the process of dying that is frightening.

Many times people who are dying need to talk about some of their fears to work through them. Some might need to hear their loved ones tell them they will be okay after they die. They may need to speak to a minister about unresolved "wrongs" from their past. They may have fears of being a burden, or "too dependent," like Morrie in *Tuesdays With Morrie*. He was dying of ALS (Lou Gehrig's disease) and talked about dreading the day when "someone's gonna have to wipe my ass"[1] because it was the "ultimate sign of dependency."[2]

So many of our fears are related to the future, and I have seen time and time again the fears that are expressed in the early stages of dying melt away into the reality of the actual experience when it occurs. In Morrie's case, he admitted it took some getting used to because "it was a complete surrender to the disease." And he felt "a little ashamed because our culture tells us we should be ashamed"[3] to have to be cleaned by others. Once he did surrender and let go of his shame, he began to enjoy his dependency and was able to actually revel in the experience of being turned, cleaned, rubbed with cream, and massaged.

A very precious woman, Maria, taught me a great deal about this. She, as many patients do, came to the dying process terrified of what would happen. She was fearful of the pain, of suffering, and of being a burden, and also terrified of what would happen to her family she was leaving behind.

Soon after she came into hospice Maria was put on an anti-anxiety medication, which was a very helpful adjunct to the emotional support she was receiving. I watched her over the next five months as she journeyed through her dying process, and about a month before she died there was a profound shift in her apparent fear of dying. Somewhere along the way she seemed to have done the introspective work that allowed her to attain great peace.

When she went into the hospital one last time, she was told, "Your cancer is in remission, but your liver has been damaged. You are in liver failure, and there is nothing we can do for you." With that, she was sent home to die. I thought she would be hysterical the next time I visited her, since that's how she had reacted previously whenever she had been critically sick. But when I walked into her room I was very surprised to find her lying very peacefully in bed. She greeted me with a smile, and in her hand was a small plastic statue of the Holy Family. In her other hand were her rosary beads, and the rosary was playing on the tape player. She turned to me and said gently, "Don't tell my children, they will be so upset, but I am ready to go and be with my Lord." She was clearly beyond fear and in a place of peace and surrender. She died peacefully three weeks later.

What I have observed again and again is that as long as we remain attached to this world and to our life, it is a struggle to die. Think of riding a river: So long as we hold onto the bank (our thoughts and fears), we struggle against the current. As soon as we let go and surrender to the flow, the struggle ceases. So it is with dying. When we surrender to the process of dying, there is an incredible inward flow of peace and grace.

VISIONING

As people withdraw from food and fluid and go into a natural fasting state, they begin to report experiences of seeing loved ones who have already died. Time and again family members have told me things like: "Oh, she's been talking to her brother who has been dead for thirty years. She's very confused." This is another instance of the caregivers and family projecting from their limited perspective what they think is going on.

To the caregiver, it may seem that the dying person is out of her head, confused, hallucinating. However, those of us who work with the dying will tell the family, "This is normal. She really is experiencing her brother." This is a process called "visioning." It is an expected occurrence as one is dying. It is observed, by hospice staff I work with, about 98 percent of the time, and it usually begins about two weeks before a person dies.

In reports of visioning, we, in hospice, find approximately 90 to 95 percent of the time the dying person mentions speaking to or seeing a loved one who has died. A small percent of the time they mention seeing a living relative, but normally they speak of seeing people who have passed on before, who seem to show up in a reassuring and supportive manner. Other reported visionings have been of angelic beings, favorite pets, strangers who seem to offer a comforting presence, or, as in Will's case, a beautiful place.

Very rarely, the vision can be a disturbing presence. If the visioning is disturbing, be supportive by inquiring about who they are seeing and why it is disturbing; then reassure them that this is a normal occurrence at this time in their life. And if the presence is truly disturbing, they can simply ask it to leave. Often they just need reassurance.

Elaine had chosen to spend her last weeks at a nursing home. During a visit about two weeks before she died, I asked her how she was doing. In a very frustrated tone she said, "Oh, I'm losing my mind. I'm seeing people who aren't really there."

I said, "Are they people you know or people you don't know?" And she replied, "Well, for the most part I don't know them."

When I asked her to tell me about the people she did know, she repeated, "For the most part, I don't know them." This told me she did not want to talk about the people she knew. I continued, "Tell me about who you are seeing." She told me, "There are these three young men, sitting up over there," and she pointed high up on the wall of her room. Not wanting to impose my value system on her experience, I asked, "Are they a comfort, or are they distressing?" Elaine said, "Oh no, they're great. I am glad they're here." She happened to be a woman who liked men and, as a rule, did not like women, so it was perfect she was seeing three young men. I said, "You can just relax. They are really here, and they are here for you. That is part of your process." She sighed with great relief and said, "Oh thank God! I thought I was losing my mind." And then she relaxed into her experience.

I once worked with a fourteen-year-old girl named Anna who was dying of cancer. She had come to the point where her breathing pattern and her very low blood pressure indicated she was very close to death, probably within twenty-four hours. We told the family they could stop turning her, since she was so close and the turning was creating great discomfort for her. Normally, a bedridden person needs to be turned every two hours to prevent pressure sores, but at that point we were no longer concerned about these developing. Twenty-four hours later she was still alive. One day later she was still there.

The dying go in and out of responsiveness while they are absorbed in their inner work; when they open their eyes you can see it: one moment their eyes will be half open and totally vacant, and then when you look again they will be completely present and able to connect with you. At one of these points of alertness, about forty-eight hours after we had stopped turning her, Anna looked at her parents and said: "Mom, Dad, I've met a man from Santa Fe, and he's dying, too. He asked me to go with him, but I told him I wasn't ready yet." Amazingly, Anna lived another day, and she did not have any sores.

Families repeatedly report these kinds of experiences, regardless of the dying person's beliefs. So it is undeniable that there are spiritual interactions taking place that are comforting and that there is spiritual assistance being given as the dying person is preparing to make the transition. If both the dying and the caregivers understand that this is expected, that nothing is going wrong—and, in fact, everything is going right when visioning happens—they can relax into it.

Edith was a frail, small, elderly woman who was days away from death, and her family wanted to make sure everything was okay. They called the nurse to check her, and as Edith and the nurse were talking, Edith, in a very weak but gruff voice, said, "I'm seeing people who aren't there. What's going on?" Her hospice nurse told her that many people have this experience before they die, of seeing people who have died before. She asked Edith if this was something she believed in. In a very strong voice Edith angrily replied, "No! That's not something I believe in! How am I supposed to know who is alive and who is dead?" Edith was not at all comforted by her experience, but she was still having it. So we must conclude that there is definitely an extrasensory experience that takes place at this stage in the dying process; there is a nonphysical awareness and an expanded consciousness.

HALLUCINATIONS/CONFUSION VERSUS VISIONING

The experience of expanded awareness and visioning among the dying is normal and expected. People who are dying are able to carry on rational conversations, as Anna and Edith did, although their energy is weak and sentences are very short. When you are with them, you know that on some level they are hearing you, and their responses make sense, even when they are only able to gesture or change their facial expression. Hallucinations, however, are rare and most often occur when a disease affects the brain or creates toxicity, as in some cases of brain cancer, severe liver disease, or a reaction to a medication.

Fred was a patient with prostate cancer that had spread to his bones. At one point, there was inflammation in his brain that was causing him to have hallucinations. These were clearly different from the spiritual experiences he had described earlier in his illness. Fred had been paralyzed from the waist down for several months. He had told his caregivers of several spiritual experiences he'd had previously, when he had become very ill from an infection and had been close to death. He was coherent when he spoke of these, and they were real and comforting to him. At times, he said, actual angels would show up, and one was named Speed Angel.

About a month after we heard about Speed Angel, Fred had an episode of agitation and confusion. He pleaded, "Get me up, get me up, I've got to get to work. I have got to get up to my desk. Help me." He was disoriented, out of touch with the fact that he was paralyzed and unable to stand or walk. His home health aide, Gigi, who was very skilled and experienced in these kinds of situations, answered, "Fred, I wish I could help you, but there is really nothing I can do for you. Is Speed Angel around?" Fred said, "Yes." Gigi said, "Okay, what I want you to do is to ask Speed Angel what you need." Then she was silent. After a few minutes of silence, she could see Fred settling down. After several more minutes she asked, "So Fred, what did Speed Angel say?"

He looked at her and said, "He told me that I'm just exactly where I need to be, and that everything is fine." Then he just settled back and fell asleep. It was quite remarkable. As we talk to people and find they are visioning, there are ways we can use the reality of these experiences to support the person, as Gigi so skillfully did. Being open to the realness of visioning allows both the living and the dying to be comforted by these expanded realities.

It is very easy to tell the difference between confusion (hallucinations) and spiritual experiences (visioning). People who are visioning make sense in their communication. Elaine, the woman who saw three young men in her room, could be very present, and her conversation was appropriate and sensible. It is as if someone who is clear and logical in one's speech and thought process were to say, "Oh, I've seen little green people." Their language is not garbled, they are not confused or restless, and they are not irrational in their thought processes. They are simply having an experience I am not having. They are present and aware of the person with whom they are talking, and are often aware that what they are seeing is different from the normal experience of living.

On the other hand, when there is nonsensical speech and restlessness, as when Fred forgot he was paralyzed, and when we cannot reach or reason with the person, then it is clearly a case of true confusion, and sometimes hallucinations. In Fred's situation, Gigi was able to use his experience of Speed Angel, a spiritual experience, to help with his disorientation. This is also a time when medications ordered by the doctor can be useful.

Labor Stage of Dying

Up to this point, I have described what I call the "pregnancy" stage of dying: the withdrawal from food, distancing from the physical world, and the inward work of the dying person. Following this is the "labor" stage. Just as labor during birth is marked by rhythmic patterns of contractions of the uterus, so is labor during dying marked by rhythmic patterns, only in this case it is in the breathing patterns.

BREATHING PATTERNS

Once someone has come to the point of not eating solid foods and drinking very little and experiencing visioning, he or she is in the early stages of the "labor" of dying. As this phase progresses it is marked by distinct changes in the person's breathing, which becomes seemingly irregular but is actually rhythmic. The person breathes, breathes, breathes, and then there is a pause in the breathing, called "apnea," which means "without breath."

Then the person starts breathing again, and then there is another pause in the breathing. This pause, or period of apnea, can last anywhere from ten seconds to a minute and a half. This phase can be very upsetting for caregivers because during the pauses it can seem as if the person has stopped breathing altogether. Family members may be on the edge of their chairs, wondering, is this the last breath?

It is very important to know that this is an expected, normal part of the labor phase of dying— it is not the time of the person's final breaths. This rhythmic pattern of apneic breathing can last a couple of hours or several days. Eventually, the dying person will move out of it and into what is called the transition phase, marked by what is described as "terminal restlessness." Finally, the person will move into a very deep, regular breathing pattern, then a shallower and slower breathing pattern. It is from this regular breathing that he or she will eventually cease to breathe. Do not be frightened by the rhythmic, apneic breathing pattern; it is normal.

NONRESPONSIVENESS VERSUS COMA

Another experience in the labor phase of dying is profound weakness that results in the dying person becoming nonresponsive. This is often mistaken for and described as "going into a coma." Yet it is important to know that in most cases a dying person does not go into a coma. A comatose person is not able to switch, at will, between being responsive and nonresponsive. The dying only seem as if they are comatose because they no longer have the life energy to respond. But they are certainly aware, able to hear, and able to process what they hear, up to the end, and are sometimes able to find the energy to respond in certain special situations, such as when a loved one arrives from afar.

Julian's father, who lived in another state, was dying and had not responded to anyone for days. When Julian arrived at his father's bedside and began talking to him, his father opened his eyes and smiled. The two were able to exchange a few words, and then the father died very peacefully. He was able to become responsive for Julian and, in fact, might well have been waiting for Julian to arrive before dying.

One way to be with people who cannot respond, for any reason, is to ask the same questions mentioned previously in the "Turning Inward" section—What are some of the things you are glad for or feel blessed about in your life? What regrets might you have? Do you now feel complete?—and then leave space for them to silently reflect. What also works well is to play some favorite music or read to them from their favorite poet or author. Many people experience a great deal of comfort in hearing passages from the Bible or readings from whatever spiritual teachings they have followed. In these ways, we can be with people who are not able to respond, and we can create an environment that is comforting and healing to their inner world and process. The closer people are to dying, the more quietly being with them supports the peaceful environment that develops in the last days and hours.

THE SENSE OF HEARING

When we are dying, hearing is the last of the physical senses to go. Everything spoken in a dying person's room must be said with the awareness that it will be heard and may affect the dying person. Many people had actually been in a coma, sometimes for years, and when they eventually awakened, they were able to describe who said what and how they had been handled by various people. So it is crucial to be aware that no matter what people's ability to respond is, or what their level of consciousness appears to be, they are able to hear. We must speak at all times as if they were fully awake and responsive.

Along the same lines, when the end is near and the dying person is too weak to respond, if a loved one cannot get there in time, it can make a vital difference for all involved if the loved one can call and the phone is put up to the person's ear. It is important that the one dying be able to listen to what the caller wants—or needs—to say. It may be the very words or connection required for letting go to be possible, or it may be what the caller needs to feel complete.

Providing gentle healing music during this time can create a supportive environment. There are musicians, often harpists or singers, available who have studied the healing effects of music on illness. These musicians can be brought into the home, many times through hospice, to play or sing specific music that is known to facilitate the dying process. These soothing sounds, of course, can also greatly benefit the caregivers and family members who are in need of comfort as well.

THE TRANSITION PHASE

During labor in childbirth, there is a time called the transition phase where the woman, just before moving into the active birthing process, feels as though she just cannot get comfortable. She is restless, feels as if she won't be able to stand the labor another minute, and is about to jump out of her skin—and then she moves into active birthing.

A similar experience happens during the dying process. After the period of rhythmic, apneic breathing, which marks the labor phase, the person moves into the transition phase or terminal restlessness. In this stage, there is usually agitation, restlessness, moaning, and groaning. The person seems quite uncomfortable.

This can be a very distressing time for loved ones because it seems as if something is going terribly wrong. It is often assumed that there has been a sudden increase in pain or discomfort and that this pain must be alleviated. Indeed, there appears to be a definite increase in discomfort compared with the peaceful state the person was in during the period of rhythmic breathing.

What is actually causing the discomfort is hard to say. From the observations of those of us who work with the dying, this stage seems to be akin to the restlessness at the end of labor. In this sense, it may be related to the confinement of the body as the dying person is trying to leave. Some spiritual teachers, in fact, have likened this restlessness to the soul's last struggle to get out of the body.

There are some effective medications that can be given at this time to help the person relax through this very agitated period. Among these are morphine and lorazepam (Ativan).

Just as with labor, the role of the one observing the process is to be supportive of the dying person through this natural phase. This is an expected, transitional stage. Nothing is going wrong. Being with them in loving presence, trusting the process, and remembering this is to be expected are some of the most effective ways to go through this time. It can be hard to watch, but it will pass. Also, giving yourself breaks from the bedside can support you in supporting them.

When I was twenty-eight, my mother was dying of pancreatic cancer. As a young nurse, to whom the natural process of death and dying had not been taught, I was unaware that she was going through predictable phases. Hospice was not available in those days to provide supportive care and information. When she started moaning and groaning, it terrified me. I was afraid something terrible was going on, she seemed to be in such pain. I didn't know what to do, and I didn't know it meant she was very close to death. I only knew she seemed in distress, and I had no idea why or how to help her. I decided I would have to take her to the hospital in the morning because caring for her was beyond anything I knew how to do at that point. She died four hours later very peacefully and easily. It would have been so helpful for me to know that the restlessness was a natural, temporary phase and an indication she was very near to death.

The Active Stage of Dying – "Deathing"

Eventually, the dying person moves out of the transition phase into the last stage of dying, a very peaceful time marked by deep regular breathing, which becomes progressively slower and shallower.

First the breathing is deep, down into the abdomen, then eventually the breath only goes to the chest, then just to the upper part of the chest. Very soon only the person's mouth and neck are moving, the mouth opening and closing in a "fish out of water" kind of breathing. Then, when the breath actually stops, you can hardly tell it has happened because it is so peaceful and easy.

Hollywood often shows a theatrical gasping for air, but that is not what happens at all. There is actually something called "the death rattle," but it is not a horrible gasping for air, and it is not at the very end. The rattling sound is caused by secretions gathering in the back of the throat because the person has become too weak to clear his or her throat. The dying person is breathing through the secretions, and caregivers may think the person is choking and needs to be suctioned in order to be able to breathe. Once again, we are projecting upon the dying person our discomfort. It is important to really see what is going on, to observe the fact that the person is breathing quite comfortably. They are not struggling for air or thrashing in the bed, "air hungry"; they are comfortable. It is crucial to realize that the discomfort is in us. It is a natural reaction to what we are hearing, since we know that if we had that much secretion in our throat we would be uncomfortable. Be assured that the people who are dying in this situation are fine. As they are leaving their body, their experience of being in their body is different from what we, from the outside, might imagine it to be.

So often the remark heard from the family after their loved one has died is, "It was so peaceful; he looked so radiant. I could hardly tell when he took his last breath." In most cases, though not all, there is deep peace at the time of death that is palpable to those at the bedside.

THE MYSTERY OF THE TIMING OF DEATH

It is clear to those who work closely with the dying that we very often choose our time of death. One of the greatest mysteries in this very complex and blessed event is how we make that choice. How is it that some individuals can leave their body easily, seemingly at the proverbial snap of their fingers, while others do not seem able to let go in spite of apparent readiness?

Violet was a cancer patient who, after months of growing weaker and gradually surrendering to her process, asked me one day: "How can I die? I am ready to go." I said, "If you are really ready to die, then it is important that you stop taking in anything whatsoever." She was already at the point where she was only drinking very small amounts. She immediately had her daughters remove all fluids from her bedside. We continued moistening her mouth for comfort and turning and tending to her. Because of her particular illness she had tremendous amounts of fluid (edema) in her body, and even with no oral intake she still lived for three weeks more, since she was being sustained by the accumulated fluid in her body. Usually it takes three to five days to die once all intake has ceased. Even though Violet seemed to have done all that was needed—she had everything taken care of, her daughters were at her bedside, she seemed to have cleared all her unfinished business and spiritual work—and felt ready, she still could not easily get out of her body. When she did die, she was very peaceful.

Another woman, Maggie, also took an amazing amount of time to die. She was a solitary soul, a very private person who had no family attachments to keep her here. Much of her dying time was spent alone, except for her dogs and a business friend who promised to be with her through the process. The friend and I could not figure out why Maggie was taking so long to die. To us, there seemed to be nothing in her life keeping her here. She finally died on August 4. Afterwards, when her friend was going through her papers, she discovered that Maggie's husband had died on August 4, fifteen years earlier. People very often hold on until a certain date: a birthday, an anniversary, a graduation, or some other date special to them.

On the other hand, some individuals are able to leave quite quickly. The mother of a very dear friend of mine had flown in from out of state to be tested to determine why she was not feeling well. She was admitted to the hospital on a Tuesday. On Wednesday, the doctors performed a biopsy that showed lung cancer. Obviously, this woman had not felt well for a while and had lost weight, but she had been able to make the flight and was still relatively strong. That night, as her family was leaving after visiting her in the hospital, they said, "Good night, Little Mama," and she replied, "Good-bye, darlins." They said, "Don't say good-bye, Little Mama, say good night." Again she replied, "Good-bye, darlin's."

At midnight, when the nurse made her rounds, Little Mama seemed to be okay. By 12:30 a.m., the next round, Little Mama had died. Elisabeth Kübler-Ross taught us about the importance of listening to the dying—but who would have thought Little Mama was that close to death?

The most common time of death is between 4:00 and 6:00 a.m., just as it is the most common time for birth. In some traditions, this is also the time when people get up to pray, meditate, or do other forms of spiritual practice. Spiritual traditions teach that this is the time when, in terms of energetics or nonphysical reality, the veil between this world and the next is thinnest. So it makes sense, given this framework, that these early morning hours are when many people come into this world and when they leave.

Some people seem to need privacy, or space, to die. They may wait until a loved one, who has been at their bedside for hours, leaves the room for a few minutes, and then they quietly let go. For others, it seems to be the opposite: they hold on until a certain person arrives, and minutes after the arrival, die. It is hard to predict how it will be for each individual.

It is very important for loved ones to not feel guilty for not being present at the time of death. Dying people choose their own time to leave. If someone you love dies without you being there, it may well be that he or she was protecting you from having to be present at the moment of death. Or it may mean they needed privacy to be able to let go, since the bonds of love and connection can hold us here when, otherwise, we are ready to move on.

There are only four kinds of people in the world—those who have been caregivers, those who currently are caregivers, those who will be caregivers, and those who will need caregivers.

— ROSALYNN CARTER

PART III

Caregiver Support

Being a Caregiver

Taking care of a loved one who is dying is among the hardest, richest, most soul-wrenching, life-changing, worthwhile work we will ever do. The challenges of the experience are unique to the course of the disease and to our loved ones' relationship to their own death. Their personal journey through their last months, days, and hours is greatly influenced by their core relationships, family, and extended support system. The caregivers' challenges are influenced by their relationship to the dying loved one, as well as their relationship to death in general.

In hospice, we say the entire family is our patient. Each family member must deal with what this experience, this loss, means to him or her. They must deal with their grief, with any unresolved situations they have involving the dying person, with how available they can be to help while still attending to the demands of daily life, and, certainly, with any other family dynamics that arise during this highly emotional and stressful time.

Family members who come to a place of acceptance with the fact that a loved one is dying can experience great gifts of intimacy during this process. The dying person often is able to be with loved ones in ways that make this time easier and, in fact, richer for all involved. There may be a greatly increased ability to give, and the chance to share the openness and honesty that people often come to in their time of dying. There is an opportunity to be together in ways that, often, neither the people who are dying nor loved ones have previously experienced.

I remember a woman named Bev who was dying of metastatic cancer that was blocking her intestines. When I first began coming to her home and needed to do any kind of physical examination, she would ask her husband of many years to step out of the room. There was clearly a distance in the relationship, which, I found out later, was related to some disappointments in their marriage over time.

As her disease progressed, Bev became bed bound and in need of increased care, which her husband, Jack, willingly provided. Soon she found that whenever she ate anything she would vomit. The food simply could not pass through her stomach. However, she still had a certain amount of appetite and desired very specific foods. So, since every time she ate she vomited, she and Jack developed a routine they called the "bucket brigade." Bev would eat and enjoy the taste and texture of the food and Jack would stand by with a paper towel–lined bowl, which she would use when the food came back up.

Over time, as Jack cared for her so willingly and lovingly, there was clearly a shift in their relationship. She no longer asked him to leave the room when anything intimate needed to be done. There was a lightness and affection that grew between them and, as they spent time reminiscing, they actually decided to write their memoirs of the summers they spent traveling through the country's national parks. The intimacy in that household at the time of Bev's death was beautiful and very moving.

For loved ones going through this process, it is important for them to receive support for their own grief that is a normal part of letting go of someone you love. Some of this grieving can be done with the dying person, depending on the level of comfort with deep emotion, while other grieving must be done away from the person who is dying. Releasing the grief is one way to find healing through this powerful experience.

There is an old Jewish saying, "Tears are for the soul what a shower is for the body." That says it all.

Caring for the Caregiver

Very often loved ones are so busy taking care of the one who is sick that they forget to tend to their own physical and emotional needs. They must be aware of those personal needs and of their response to what is happening, and remember they need support as well. This includes eating healthy food, taking breaks away from the bedside, exercising, doing things that are personally nourishing, as well as being with loved ones who are supportive. As caregivers give support to someone who is dying, they need to have others giving them support for their process of physical, emotional, and spiritual caregiving as they are saying good-bye to their loved one.

So often near the end people who are dying only want their core people around. This can be a very intense time for the caregivers. It is important to use your support system to lighten your load regarding external concerns, like shopping, errand running, returning phone calls, tending to the garden, or caring for the pets, so that you have the energy to be present at the sacred event that is unfolding.

Hospice

Many families do not want to request hospice services because they see it as a death sentence for their loved one. Or they believe hospice is only to be called when the dying person is bed bound and does not have much time left. Nothing is further from the truth. Hospice should be called as soon as the patient, the family, and their doctor have determined the family member is probably counting his or her life in months rather than years, and the decision has been made to no longer pursue curative treatment. Hospice services are usually covered by insurance, Medicaid, or Medicare, and if none of those are options, the hospice will work with you to provide services.

People need to know that while the main focus of hospice is caring for patients who are dying, the broader realm of hospice expertise is working with clients with life-threatening illnesses. Whether or not death occurs, certain issues come up when individuals are seriously ill. Hospice can help in cases where the disease process is life threatening and the physician involved believes, assuming the progression of the disease continues as it has, the person has months rather than years of life remaining. If it turns out the person gets better—that it is not yet time to die after all—great! They "graduate" from hospice, and off they go.

One of my first patients in Santa Fe was put on hospice care with a terminal cancer diagnosis after his initial treatment did not seem to change the progression of his cancer. He was on hospice for three months and then, much to our and his physician's amazement, started to improve. Subsequently, he graduated from hospice. I saw him at the farmers' market nine years later, and he said, "It's so good to see you. I told you I'd make it!" And he had. Through the power of prayer, a loving family, a strong will, faith, chemotherapy, and the fact that it was not his time to leave, he survived. For other people who do all these same things and die, clearly it is their time to die.

Hospice doctors and nurses are experts at pain and symptom management, at determining what is causing the pain or discomfort and knowing how to treat it. When people are in a hospice, the nurses closely monitor the patients and their progression two to three times a week or more often if needed. If a family member has a concern between nursing visits, a nurse is on call twenty-four hours a day. In this way, the family always has access to a clinician to help with any problem that might come up. The nurse then has the support and backup from the hospice physician in case the patient's doctor is unavailable for any reason.

There are also home health aides who will come in for a few hours a day, usually three times a week, to help with personal care and light housekeeping. It is important to know that these aides are not available for extended shifts. That level of caregiving, if unable to be met by family, friends, and volunteer support, must be addressed by private hire home health aides or placement in an inpatient hospice or other care facility.

There are also social workers who provide support for the emotional needs of the family and friends who are the primary support team, as well as help the family attend to the logistics of legal concerns such as a living will and durable power of attorney.

There are spiritual care coordinators, or chaplains, who provide nondenominational support whenever spiritual issues need to be addressed.

Then there are the invaluable volunteers without whom hospice cannot be done in the way it is meant to be. There is a volunteer coordinator who assigns volunteers to be there for families as only volunteers can. They are able to come and stay with the patient for a few or up to several hours to give the family time away from the home, or they can run errands for family members who do not wish to leave the bedside. Additionally, they are available to help with whatever creative or unique needs their assigned patient and family may have.

After the death, there is often a volunteer assigned for the first year of bereavement to keep in contact with the caregivers for any support that is needed.

Hospice is one of the most important support systems available through this challenging, gift-filled event. So often the families tell us that, in retrospect, they wish they had requested hospice earlier than they did.

What Kind of Help Really Helps?

When you are called to go through this experience with a loved one and wish to help, the most important thing you can do—while making sure the person is as safe and as comfortable as possible—is listen to the dying person. Let the person take the lead. Some people want to be active and conscious in the midst of their dying process, while others do not. Some desire to be alert; some prefer to stay sedated. Some people want to talk about their process, but others do not. So it is all about allowing people to be where they are. At the same time, allow yourself to be present with what is, rather than getting caught up in your fears or desires for what might be. One woman insightfully told me she realized she had spent so much time trying to "do" the right thing that she missed "being" present with her loved one.

I had to relearn this lesson with my father. He was a doctor, a surgeon, and he was dying, basically of starvation, as a result of having undergone ulcer surgery thirty years before, which removed 50 percent of his stomach. Over the years, what little was left did not absorb food well. He had been hospitalized for severe weakness.

It was clear to me he was dying. I could see the weight loss and overall decrease in life energy. I stayed in the hospital with him every night for about a week before he died. At one point, I said, "Daddy, do you have the sense that you are dying?" He just looked at me and furiously replied, "Hell no, I'm not dying! Well, of course everybody is dying, but I'm not dying anytime soon." (He had always been quick to anger.) And I thought, "Okay, clearly we are not going down that road." Then I asked, "What about your funeral? What do you want to happen when you do die?" And, surprisingly, he could talk about that at length.

That is one of the ways we can be with people who are dying: go with what they want to talk about, not what you want to. One point to cover is what kind of services they would like and how they would like to be remembered. Many times they will want to plan their own funeral or memorial service. That is what my dad did. He talked about his funeral in detail, choosing such aspects as the place, the music, and the readings.

You can ask the dying person questions, and by listening to the responses you will come to know what he or she wants to talk about and what is important in their remaining time. In this way, you can provide the greatest possible support.

Assisted Suicide

In my experience a very small percent, perhaps 5 percent, of the United States population want to have the means to end their life when it gets to be "too much" or when they feel they have become too great a burden. Interestingly, according to a study published by the American Medical Association, less than 1 percent actually follow through with their plan.[1] Evidently people want to know they have some control over when they die. Yet very few seem to reach a point where life becomes too much to bear. The vast majority of people find that the unbearable suffering they anticipated does not happen, and they die a natural and peaceful death. As one dying woman told me, "I keep waiting for it to get awful and it doesn't."

As for the relatively small number of people who wish to hasten their demise, there is a ready solution: they can simply stop eating and drinking. In a body that has already begun shutting down, the resulting biochemical state, as described earlier, promotes a comfortable and harmonious transition. Ultimately, the means to end one's life need not consist of illegal acts, toxic levels of medications, or other forms of active suicide. The often-overlooked natural alternative—opting for a withdrawal of nutrition and hydration— is far more peace inducing.

My hope for those thinking of suicide at the end of their life is that they have hospice care for at least a month before pursuing their plan, so that the concerns and fears that caused them to consider this can be addressed and eased.

Sudden Death

Sudden death, unlike the natural, gradual passage we can come to understand, remains more of a mystery.

Many people who have lived through the sudden death of a loved one tell me their loved one, subsequently, contacted them, often through a dream, a vision, or the emanation of a strong fragrance. My sense is those who die suddenly find themselves in that greater realm as described in the "Visioning" section. It is as if they have had an out-of-body experience, only they do not come back into their body. They then often find ways to be in touch with loved ones to ease the pain of sudden separation.

The movie *Ghost* portrays this well. It is about a man who is stabbed and dies suddenly. He then finds he is having an out-of-body experience, only he soon realizes he is no longer alive and able to function on the physical plane even though he can perceive it. He must instead adjust to being dead. This film, despite being a Hollywood depiction of sudden death, seems to parallel interactions people have reported to me after the sudden loss of a loved one.

The out-of-body experience itself has been described repeatedly by people who have been jolted out of their bodies. An article by Joy Allen titled "There Are No Edges to My Loving Now" chronicles her personal journey after she and her husband were in an automobile accident and both went up to the Light.

Joy was told she had to come back and her husband would stay. Returning to her body, she woke up in the intensive care unit knowing he was dead but still affected by her out-of-body experience. She recounted being in a blissful "state of grace."[2] Nine days after her return, the reality of her loss emerged and for a full year kept her "wrenched between the pain and the ecstasy."[3] The force sustaining her in the times she did not want to be alive was the driving need to find purpose for her return.

Whether Joy's near-death account resembles the out-of-body experience associated with sudden death cannot be determined. Her experiences as a survivor, however, are widely shared in accounts by others. Returning to her physical body meant not only recovering from the trauma and suffering caused by the accident but also coping with the trauma and suffering caused by the sudden death of her beloved spouse. Joy had the comfort of knowing where her husband was, while still mourning the loss of him in her life.

Grief counselors often note that the sudden death of a loved one leaves the survivors bereft, complicated by the absence of those healing opportunities that arise during the more gradual natural passage, such as the chance to say, "I love you," "please forgive me," "I forgive you," and "good-bye."

A Different View of Suffering

Dying is usually not about having to withstand tremendous physical, emotional, or spiritual suffering. On the contrary, the many dying people I have been with have taught me that we humans tend to get caught in suffering most when we are enmeshed in life as we know it and when we first begin coming to terms with the fact that it is ending. Later, as our dying gradually unfolds, we come to terms with our suffering and begin resolving fears and concerns. During the final phases of dying, we are given the opportunity to heal through unresolved reactions and fears, and toward the very end, during our final days, it appears that any existing suffering lifts about 98 percent of the time.

Sean, for example, was forty two years old, sick with polyarteritis, a very rare disease, that caused inflammation in all his arteries, resulting in poor circulation to his muscles, nervous system, and organs, which led, in turn, to progressive paralysis. Sean had been fighting this disease for a long time, and certainly there had been times of suffering for all involved, especially his wife of three years, Elena, and their three-year-old son, Israel. Over this period of time he had gone from being exceptionally active and vital to being so sapped of strength he could not sip water without Elena holding the drinking glass to his mouth.

On the day of their initial hospice visit, Sean was focused on trying to figure out how to get into his wheelchair to go to the bathroom. Elena gently and compassionately said to him, "You don't need to get into the wheelchair to go to the bathroom anymore. We really have to face the facts. This is coming to an end, and we're not going to beat this paralysis." Over the next several minutes together, they lovingly came to a place of new focus. For some time Elena and Israel had been sleeping upstairs, with Sean downstairs to make his care easier. Now she decided, enough running up and down the stairs—it is time for this family to come together.

The next day Elena moved the family bed into the living room and set Israel's bed right next to it. In their converted living room, Israel would climb up on the beds to play, then get close to his father and say, "Daddy, I'm really going to miss you." Sean, in turn, would say, "I'm really going to miss you, too." Coming together in this way profoundly enriched their last days as a family.

At Sean's memorial, someone described a gathering at his bedside one evening, when the presence of love and the sacred had been palpable. Sean had looked up and said, "You know, there are really only two emotions in the world. One is love, and the other is fear." He added, "I've spent most of my life, until recently, in fear. I know now what it is like to live in love, and it is really the only place to be." No longer was he suffering. As much as he had wanted to remain alive to be with his wife and son, he had surrendered to the truth of his dying and, in so doing, began radiating love and grace to everyone who came to be with him. That is how he died.

From Sean I witnessed once again that dying does not mean going off into a void, but it is instead the last, most important thing we do in our lives. It is a time of reflection and life review, of embracing both the joys and the regrets, and of saying good-bye to those we love most in the world. If it also happens to be a time of suffering, most of it can be alleviated through good hospice care. Medications, procedures, and equipment can be brought in to address the effects of physical discomfort. Counseling and support can help ease emotional or spiritual concerns. Among dying individuals relieved of the distresses of the physical body, a deep authenticity often emerges creating an intimacy that may have been missing for years.

This different view of suffering accepts that while it may be a part of dying in the beginning, in the majority of cases distress actually resolves, rather than increases, as people move into their last days. Eventually, when one is able to surrender into the inevitable, gradually disconnecting from the body and events on the physical plane, any preconceived boundaries we might envision between life and death dissolve.

Reflections on Living with Dying

If I had one gift to give the world, it would be to let people know death is not a failure and dying is not something to be feared. It is a natural event with predictable stages. It is part of the cycle of life. The dying person is being supported on so many levels we cannot see. Much of our perceived suffering at the bedside is within us, not within our loved one.

Dying is hard work, challenging on all levels, for all involved, and yet it is also an experience unlike any other, filled with blessings, offering life-changing opportunities for all involved.

My dear friend Pepper's mother was dying in a nursing home in California. Her grown children were with her. I was staying in touch by phone, doing hospice long distance. One day I called and her daughter Katerin came to the phone and described her mother's breathing. From the description, I recognized she was in the advanced labor of dying, so I described the stages her mother would be going through in her remaining hours. It took all of about twenty minutes to explain this. Later Katerin sent me the following note that has meant so much and says it all:

"I can't even begin to tell you how instrumental you were in helping me embrace my mom's dying process in love and release. I am so grateful for your call to the convalescent center and your quick walk-through of the physical process. Right before you called I was ready to leave, very afraid of what was going to happen. Your words gave me strength, and I was able to be present for my mom and love her through her accomplishment.

"She was so loving and courageous in return. I will never fear death and have been forever altered by that mysterious event. I am so grateful to you.

"Thank you seems so feeble an expression. In James Joyce's words, it was an epiphany."

My dream is that everyone be able to find the support allowing the fear of dying to be replaced by a richer, more positive experience that embraces the gifts available during this extraordinary time.

Dying doesn't prevent thriving. Death ends life, but dying is a crucial transitional time in our living. One of my fellow cancer patients said, "I used to think so many things were so terribly important. Now that I am doing it, I think dying is probably the most important thing we do with our lives. I really can't think of a more important time to learn to thrive."

— PAUL PEARSALL, MD

Notes

INTRODUCTION

1. "NHPCO's Facts and Figures — 2005 Findings," National Hospice and Palliative Care Organization, Alexandria, VA, November 2006.

PART I

1. Stephen Levine, interview by Eliot Rosen, *Conscious Dying: Preparing Now for a Healing Passage, the Transition We Call Death* (El Rito, New Mexico: For a World We Choose Foundation, 1996), video.

PART II

1. Mitch Albom, *Tuesdays with Morrie* (New York: Doubleday, 1997), p. 22.
2. Ibid., p. 49.
3. Ibid., p. 115.

PART III

1. Ezekiel J. Emanuel, "Euthanasia and Physician-Assisted Suicide: A Review of the Empirical Data from the United States," *Archives of Internal Medicine* 162, no. 2 (January 28, 2002).
2. Joy Allen, "There Are No Edges to My Loving Now," *Spiritual Emergence Network Newsletter,* no date available.
3. Ibid.

Resources

Further Reading

BOOKS

Albom, Mitch. *Tuesdays with Morrie: An Old Man, a Young Man, and Life's Greatest Lesson.* New York: Doubleday, 1997.

Blackman, Sushila. *Graceful Exits: How Great Beings Die.* Trumbull, CT: Weatherhill, 1997.

Byock, Ira. *Dying Well: The Prospect for Growth at the End of Life.* New York: Riverhead Press, 1997.

Callahan, Maggie, and Patricia Kelley. *Final Gifts: Understanding the Special Awareness, Needs, and Communication of the Dying.* New York: Bantam, 1992.

Capossela, Cappy, and Sheila Warnock. *Share the Care: How to Organize a Group to Care for Someone Who Is Seriously Ill.* New York: Simon & Shuster, 1995.

Dalai Lama. *Advice on Dying: And Living a Better Life.* New York: Atria Books, 2002.

Doka, Kenneth J., Bruce Jennings, and Charles A. Corr, eds. *Living with Grief: Ethical Dilemmas at the End of Life.* Washington, DC: Hospice Foundation of America, 2005.

Dossey, Larry. *The Extraordinary Healing Power of Ordinary Things.* New York: Harmony Books, 2006.

Also by Larry Dossey: *Healing Beyond the Body: Medicine and the Infinite Reach of the Mind, Healing Words: The Power of Prayer and the Practice of Medicine. Meaning and Medicine. Beyond Illness. Space, Time, and Medicine.*

Duda, Deborah. *Coming Home: A Guide to Dying at Home with Dignity.* Santa Fe, NM: Aurora, 1997.

Kessler, David. *The Rights of the Dying: A Companion for Life's Final Moments.* New York: HarperCollins, 1997.

RESOURCES

Kübler-Ross, Elisabeth. *On Death and Dying.* New York: MacMillan Publishing Co., 1969.

Also by Elisabeth Kübler-Ross: *To Live Until We Say Good-bye. On Children and Death, The Wheel of Life.*

Levine, Stephen. *A Year to Live: How to Best Live This Year as If It Were Your Last.* New York: Bell Tower, 1997.

Lynn, Joanne, and Joan Harrold. *Handbook for Mortals: Guidance for People Facing Serious Illness.* New York: Oxford Univ. Press, 1999.

Malkin, Gary Remal, and Michael Stillwater. *Graceful Passages: A Companion for Living and Dying.* Novato, CA: Companion Arts, 2000.

O'Kelly, Eugene. *Chasing Daylight: How My Forthcoming Death Transformed My Life.* New York: McGraw-Hill, 2006.

Pearsall, Paul. *The Beethoven Factor: The New Positive Psychology of Hardiness, Happiness, Healing, and Hope.* Charlottesville, VA: Hampton Roads Publishing Co., Inc. 2003.

Sapienza, Jerral. *Urgent Whispers: Care of the Dying.* Eugene, OR: L L X Press, 2002.

Sogyal Rinpoche. *The Tibetan Book of Living and Dying.* New York: HarperCollins, 1992.

Wilber, Ken. *Grace and Grit: Spirituality and Healing in the Life and Death of Treya Killam Wilber.* Boston: Shambhala Publications, 2001.

AUDIO–CD

Estes, Clarissa Pinkola. *The Radiant Coat.* Louisville, CO: Sounds True, 2006.

Malkin, Gary Remal and Michael Stillwater. *Graceful Passages: A Companion for Living and Dying.* Novato, CA: Companion Arts, 2000.

ARTICLE

Allen, Joy. "There Are No Edges to My Loving Now." *Spiritual Emergence Network Newsletter.* Date unavailable.

Emanuel, Ezekiel J. "Euthanasia and Physician-Assisted Suicide: A Review of the Empirical Data from the United States." *Archives of Internal Medicine* 162, no. 2, January 28, 2002.

VIDEO/DVD

Adair, Camille, and Grant Taylor. *Solace: Wisdom of the Dying.* Santa Fe, NM: Point of Light Productions, 2008.

Rosen, Elliott. *Conscious Dying: Preparing Now for a Healing Passage.* El Rito, NM: For a World We Choose Foundation, 1996. Video.

ORGANIZATIONS

Academy of Hospice Nurses
32478 Dunford Road
Farmington Hills, MI 48334
Phone: 303-432-5482

Access to End-of-Life Care
1351 24th Avenue
San Francisco, CA 94122
Phone: 415-566-9710
www.access2eolcare.org

Aging with Dignity
PO Box 1661
Tallahassee, FL 32302-1661
Phone: 888-594-7437
www.agingwithdignity.org

American Cancer Society
1599 Clifton Road NE
Atlanta, GA 30329
Phone: 800-227-2345
www.cancer.org

Americans for Better Care of the Dying
1700 Diagonal Road, Suite 635
Alexandria, VA 22314
Phone: 703-647-8505
www.abcd-caring.org

Association for Death Education and Counseling
60 Revere Drive, Suite 500
Northbrook, IL 60062
Phone: 847-509-0403

Five Wishes
PO Box 1661
Tallahassee, FL 32302-1661
Phone: 888-594-7437
www.agingwithdignity.org

Hospice Foundation of America (HFA)
1621 Connecticut Avenue NW, Suite 300
Washington, DC 20009
Phone: 800-854-3402 or 202-638-5419
www.hospicefoundation.org

National Hospice and Palliative Care Organization
1700 Diagonal Road, Suite 635
Alexandria, VA 22314
Phone: 703-837-1500
www.nhpco.org

WEB SITES
Beliefnet
www.beliefnet.com

Dying Well
www.dyingwell.org

Final Thoughts
www.finalthoughts.com

Living through Dying
www.livingthroughdying.com

On Our Own Terms
www.thirteen.org/onourownterms

About the Author

Denys (pronounced *De-knee*) Cope is a registered nurse, end-of-life coach, educator, healthcare consultant, ordained minister, and counselor specializing in the dying process, eldercare (including Alzheimer's disease), and end-of-life issues.

She has a bachelor of science in nursing from California State University at Chico and a master's in spiritual science degree from the Peace Theological Seminary and College of Philosophy.

Denys has journeyed with the dying and their families for most of her adult life. As a registered nurse since 1966, a hospice nurse since 1984, and an end-of-life coach since 2002, she has midwifed the passage of hundreds of people. She is known for her compassion and strength in guiding the dying and their loved ones through what most people believe is a difficult and painful experience. Denys believes that the dying process is the most important event in our lives and offers lectures and workshops to raise awareness of it, as well as related topics.

Denys currently lives in Santa Fe, New Mexico, with her two cats, amid a community of dear friends savoring "The Land of Enchantment."

To learn more about her work, visit
www.denyscope.com